CAMBRIDGE
UNIVERSITY PRESS

CB081718

Cambridge Grammar and Writing Skills

Learner's Book 4

Wendy Wren and Sarah Lindsay

CAMBRIDGE
UNIVERSITY PRESS

Shaftesbury Road, Cambridge CB2 8EA, United Kingdom

One Liberty Plaza, 20th Floor, New York, NY 10006, USA

477 Williamstown Road, Port Melbourne, VIC 3207, Australia

314–321, 3rd Floor, Plot 3, Splendor Forum, Jasola District Centre, New Delhi – 110025, India

103 Penang Road, #05-06/07, Visioncrest Commercial, Singapore 238467

Cambridge University Press is part of the University of Cambridge.

It furthers the University's mission by disseminating knowledge in the pursuit of education, learning and research at the highest international levels of excellence.

www.cambridge.org
Information on this title: www.cambridge.org/9781108730624

20 19 18 17 16 15 14 13 12

Printed in Poland by Opolgraf

A catalogue record for this publication is available from the British Library

ISBN 978-1-108-73062-4 Paperback

Name ....

Class ....

Date ....

I can write: ✓

UNIT 1	Writing to communicate: book blurbs	....
UNIT 2	Narrative writing: characters in stories	....
UNIT 3	Poetry: acrostics and haikus	....
UNIT 4	Factual writing: reports	....
UNIT 5	Narrative writing: dialogue in stories	....
UNIT 6	Instructional writing: recipes	....
UNIT 7	Writing to persuade: advertisements	....
UNIT 8	Personal writing: recounts	....
UNIT 9	Narrative writing: play scripts	....

Contents

Teacher guided writing **Let's practise**	Independent writing **Let's write**	Resource sheets
• Book blurb for the story *The Mouse and the Lion* • Book blurb for non-fiction book *Everything You Need to Know About Cricket*	• Book blurb for own choice of story • Book blurb for own choice of non-fiction book	• Present tenses • Creating a book blurb
• Character description of another character in the story extract	• Character description of another character in the extract	• Past tenses • Adjectives • Creating a character
• An acrostic poem using the words A SUNNY DAY • A haiku from picture stimulus	• An acrostic poem using the words THE MOON • A haiku from picture stimulus	• Vocabulary reference list • Creating an acrostic
• Factual report on the Petronas Twin Towers from given source material	• Factual report for own choice of building	• Past and present tenses • Writing from notes
• Conversation in the next part of the story from a given scenario	• Characters talking about football from a given scenario	• Punctuating dialogue • Synonyms • Creating a dialogue

Unit	Reading **Let's read**	Comprehension **Let's talk**	Writing features **Let's learn**
6	Instructional writing: recipes	• What does the recipe tell you? • Thinking about recipes • How is a recipe written?	• Headings and sub-headings • Imperative verbs • Adverbs • Sentences • Precise language • Layout
7	Writing to persuade: advertisements	• What does the advertisement tell you? • Thinking about advertisements • How is an advertisement created?	• Adjectives • Information • Rhyme • Alliteration • Quotations • Layout
8	Personal writing: recounts	• What does the recount tell you? • Thinking about the personal recount • How is a personal recount written?	• Introduction • Pronouns – first person • Past tenses • Reported speech • Order • Fact and opinion
9	Narrative writing: play scripts	• What happens in the play? • What do we learn about the characters? • How is a play script written?	• Contractions • Dialogue • Layout

Teacher guided writing **Let's practise**	Independent writing **Let's write**	Resource sheets
• Constructing a recipe from continuous prose	• Constructing a recipe from continuous prose	• Adverbs • Creating a recipe
• Creating an advertisement for a drink	• Creating an advertisement from a choice of products	• Adjectives • Creating an advertisement
• Recounting a class visit	• Recounting a visit with family or friends	• Reported speech
• The next scene of the pay from a given scenario	• The next scene of the pay from a given scenario	• Contractions • Layout

1 Writing to communicate: book blurbs

You will find a **blurb** on the back cover of a book.

A book blurb is written to tell readers what the book is about.

Let's read

Fiction book blurbs

Read this blurb for a fiction book called *Leila's Game*.

Leila loves sport. She loves basketball. She watches every game her classmates play. She cannot play herself because she is in a wheelchair.

She sits at the side. She cheers but the team always loses! Miss Garcia, the coach, cannot understand it.

Every Saturday, Leila plays board games with her grandfather. He tells her he always has a plan for how he will play any game. This gives Leila an idea. She thinks of a plan for the next game. She tells Miss Garcia and the team.

Will Leila's plan work?

Will the team win their next game?

This is a lovely story of friendship and never giving up, with a very unexpected ending. It will keep you turning the pages!

Let's talk

A What does the book blurb tell you? Discuss your answers.

1 What does Leila love?

2 Why can't Leila play basketball?

3 Who is Miss Garcia?

4 What does Leila do every Saturday?

5 What does her grandfather say that gives Leila an idea?

6 Who does Leila tell about her idea?

B Think about book blurbs. Discuss your answers.

1 Why do you think books have blurbs?

2 What does the blurb for *Leila's Game* tell you?

3 What does it not tell you?

4 Why do you think the blurb includes questions?

C How is a book blurb written? Discuss your answers.

1 Look at the verbs in the book blurb, for example:

loves *watches* *cheers*

What tense are they written in?

2 Are the sentences

a short and simple?

b long and complicated?

3 Is the blurb

a very long?

b very short?

Let's learn

Sentences

A book blurb needs to be **short** and **simple**.

Readers want to know **quickly** if it is the sort of book they would like to read.

A book blurb mainly uses **short sentences**.
Leila loves sport. She loves basketball.

Top Tip

Remember your capital letters and full stops.

A Write this long sentence as three short sentences.

The basketball team always loses because they have no plan, but Leila has an idea.

Sentence 1: ____________________

Sentence 2: ____________________

Sentence 3: ____________________

Present tenses

Book blurbs are written in **present tenses**.

Verbs have different **tenses**: **past**, **present** and **future**.

Past tenses:	Leila **watched**	Leila **was watching**
Present tenses:	Leila **watches**	Leila **is watching**
Future tense:	Leila **will watch**	

A Write these past tense sentences in the present tense.

1 Leila talked to her grandfather.

____

2 He gave her an idea.

____

3 She told Miss Garcia about her plan.

____

Questions

Book blurbs often use **questions**.

Questions end with a **question mark**.
Will Leila's plan work?

A Write these sentences as questions.

1 Leila likes watching basketball.

____

2 Miss Garcia is the team coach.

____

3 Leila has a plan.

____

B Answer these questions about book blurbs.

1 Use the first few sentences to let the reader know what the book is about.

What is *Leila's Game* about?

____

2 Always put the names of the main characters in your blurb.

Who are the three main characters in *Leila's Game*?

_______________ _______________ _______________

3 Never give away the ending of the story. Why not?

____

____

4 Use questions to keep the reader guessing.

Find and copy an example of a question in the blurb for *Leila's Game*.

____

____

Let's practise

This short story was written a long, long time ago.

The Mouse and the Lion

One day, Lion was sleeping in the jungle. He was woken by Mouse hunting for food. Lion grabbed Mouse and was going to eat her. Mouse asked Lion to spare her. Mouse said that one day, she might be able to help Lion. Lion laughed and laughed. How could a tiny, weak mouse ever help strong, fierce Lion? He thought it was so funny that he let Mouse go.

Some time later, Lion was caught by hunters. They tied him to a tree. They would come back later and kill him. Mouse was hunting for food and heard Lion roaring. She found Lion tied to a tree by strong ropes. Mouse began to gnaw at the ropes. Soon Lion was free.

Lion thanked Mouse. He was glad that he hadn't eaten her!

Writing book blurbs

You are going to write a **book blurb** for the story *The Mouse and the Lion.*

A Planning

Use the questions below to help you plan your blurb. Make notes.

1 How will you begin your blurb? Choose one of these or use your own idea. Write your first sentence.

One day... This is a story about... Do you think...?

____

2 Think about your first few sentences. Make sure you mention the main characters, Mouse and Lion. What is Lion doing? What is Mouse doing?

____

____

____

____

3 What is Lion going to do to Mouse?

____

____

4 What does Mouse say?

____

____

5 When do Lion and Mouse meet again?

____

____

6 Which part of the story will you leave out of your blurb?

____

____

7 What questions could you ask at the end of the blurb?

____

____

B Writing

Now use your notes to write your book blurb.

Writer's Toolbox

Have you:

- included the **main points** of the story?
- mentioned the **main characters**?
- written in **present tenses**?
- kept your blurb **short**?
- mainly used **short sentences**?
- not given away the **ending**?
- ended the blurb with **a question**?

Edit and proofread

Correct mistakes in: spelling punctuation grammar

Write your neat copy.

Let's write

You are going to write a blurb for a story.

A Planning

1 Choose a story that you like and know well. Write the title of the story.

____

2 Who are the main characters?

_______________ _______________ _______________

3 Make notes on what happens in the story.

____

____

____

____

4 Write the first sentence of your blurb.

____

____

5 You are **not** going to give away the story ending, so what question could you write at the end of the blurb?

____

____

B Writing

Now use your notes to write your book blurb.

Writer's Toolbox

Have you:

- included the **main points** of the story?
- mentioned the **main characters**?
- written in **present tenses**?
- kept your blurb **short**?
- mainly used **short sentences**?
- not given away the **ending**?
- ended the blurb with **a question**?

Edit and proofread

Correct any mistakes in: spelling   punctuation   grammar

Write your neat copy.

Let's read

Non-fiction book blurbs

Book blurbs appear on the back of **non-fiction** books as well.

Read this blurb for a non-fiction book called *Let's Go Diving*.

Have you ever wondered what it would be like to dive under the sea?

Then this is the book for you!

Diving is a very popular sport. The author explains what you can see under the waves. You can see coral reefs, marine life and even shipwrecks! He describes the different ways of diving. He describes the equipment you need. He charts the history of diving from the heavy diving suits of the past to the scuba tanks that divers use today.

Chapters such as *Exploring Shipwrecks* and *Extreme Diving* show how exciting, and also dangerous, this sport can be!

The book includes colourful, interesting pictures. It has a helpful glossary that explains terms used in diving.

Let's talk

A What does the book blurb tell you? Discuss your answers.

1 What is the book about?

2 What can you see under the waves?

3 What equipment did divers use in the past?

4 What equipment do divers use today?

5 Give an example of a chapter heading.

6 What interesting and helpful things does the author include?

B Think about book blurbs. Discuss your answers.

1 What question does the blurb begin with?

2 Why do you think the blurb begins with this question?

3 What details about diving does the blurb tell you?

4 Do you think the blurb tells you everything that is in the book? Why? Why not?

5 After reading the blurb, would you like to read this book? Why? Why not?

C How is a book blurb written? Discuss your answers.

1 Look at the verbs in the book blurb, for example:

is *explains* *describes*

What tense are they written in?

2 Are the sentences

a short and simple?

b long and complicated?

3 Is the blurb

a very long?

b very short?

Let's learn

Sentences

Both fiction and non-fiction blurbs need to be **short** and **simple**.

Readers want to know quickly if this is the sort of book they would like to read.

Blurbs use **short sentences**.

A Find and copy a short sentence from the blurb.

____

Present tenses

Blurbs are written in **present tenses**.

*Leila **is watching** a game of basketball.* *Diving **is** a very popular sport.*

A Find three examples of present tenses in the blurb for *Let's Go Diving.*

1 ____________ 2 ____________ 3 ____________

Questions

Both fiction and non-fiction blurbs often use **questions** to capture the reader's interest.

Questions end with a **question mark**.

A Find and copy a question from the blurb.

____

Non-fiction book blurbs

- Blurbs for non-fiction books must explain what the book is about.
- It must give details that will interest the reader.
- Non-fiction books do not have an ending that the blurb must not give away.

A Make notes.

1 What you can see: coral reefs marine life ____________

2 Equipment of the past: ____________

3 Today's equipment: ____________

4 Exciting chapters: ____________

Let's practise

Here is the contents page for a book called *Everything You Need to Know About Cricket.*

Contents

You are going to write a **book blurb** for the book *Everything You Need to Know About Cricket.*

A Planning

Use the questions below to help you plan your blurb. Make notes.

1 What question could you ask your reader at the start of the blurb?

____

2 What short sentence could you write about Chapter 1? You could include:

long trousers helmet bat

____

____

3 What short sentence could you write about Chapter 2? You could include:

Test matches One-day games Twenty20

____

____

4 Which famous cricketers could you mention? You could include:

Sarfraz Ahmed Sachin Tendulkar Alastair Cook

____

____

B Writing

Now use your notes to write your book blurb.

Writer's Toolbox

Have you:

- started your blurb with **a question**?
- mainly used **short sentences**?
- written in **present tenses**?
- included **interesting details**?
- kept your blurb **short**?

Edit and proofread

Correct any mistakes in: spelling punctuation grammar

Write your neat copy.

Let's write

You are going to write a blurb for a non-fiction book.

A Planning

1 Choose a non-fiction book that you found interesting. Write the title.

____

2 What question are you going to begin with?

____

3 Make notes on the chapter headings you are going to include in your blurb and the details from the book you are going to include in your blurb.

B Writing

Now use your notes to write your book blurb.

- Use the **Writer's Toolbox**, above.
- **Edit and proofread**, correcting any mistakes in **spelling**, **punctuation** and **grammar**, and then write your neat copy.

2 Narrative writing: characters in stories

Characters are usually people or animals in a story.

We need to know:

- what a character **looks like**
- what **sort of person** that character is.

Let's read

Read this extract from a story called *Rescue!* We find out a lot about Len.

Rescue!

The story so far…

Len is a firefighter. It is a dangerous job and people think of him as a real-life hero. In the first chapter of the story, Len has rescued people from a burning building. It is now the weekend and Len is enjoying his time off.

It was a Saturday morning early in June, and Len decided to work in his garden. He dressed quickly in patched jeans and an old T-shirt. By the back door, he pulled on his muddy boots and gardening gloves, and put a baseball cap on his curly, black hair.

He stepped into the garden and went into his shed. He kept his gardening tools there. They were hanging neatly on hooks or lined up on the workbench. He took down a large rake and went to a part of the garden that was overgrown. Len began to work. He was fit and strong, so he soon cleared the tangled weeds and rubbish.

Grace, his wife, came into the garden. She was carrying a mug of steaming tea for her husband. "You're getting on well," she said, looking at the cleared patch of soil. "We'll soon have our pond."

"Yes," said Len, looking pleased with his work. He drank his tea. "What are you doing today?"

"I'm marking Year 4's stories," she said. "The children have worked so hard, I want to give the stories back on Monday morning."

"Have fun," said Len, as Grace went back into the house.

"Right," thought Len. "The next job is to dig a big hole!"

Len got a wheelbarrow from the shed and pushed it to the cleared patch. He began to dig, humming happily to himself as he was working. Soon the heavy wheelbarrow was full, but he easily pushed it behind the shed where he emptied it. Len worked steadily as he was determined to finish the hole before he went in for lunch. The hole got bigger and bigger. The pile of soil grew and grew. Len had almost finished. One more full wheelbarrow should do it.

Just then, Mrs Brown appeared at the gate. She was a neighbour who lived next door in Bank Street. "Len!" she cried. Len put down the spade and jumped quickly out of the hole.

"What's the matter?" he asked. He could see that Mrs Brown was upset and he wanted to help. "What's happened?"

"It's Saska," she said. "She's stuck up a tree and that horrible dog from across the road is barking at her. I'm sorry to bother you on your day off," she said politely. "Will you help?"

"Of course," replied Len. "Of course I'll help. Don't worry. I'll soon have her down."

Grace heard voices and came out hurriedly to see what was going on. Len explained and went into the shed to get his ladder.

"No rest for heroes!" said Grace.

Let's talk

A What happens in the story? Discuss your answers.

1 What day is it?

2 What does Len decide to do?

3 What does he keep in the shed?

4 What does Len take from the shed?

5 What does Grace bring for Len?

6 What is Len doing in the garden?

7 Who comes into the garden when Len has nearly finished?

8 What has happened to Saska?

B What do you learn about Len? Discuss your answers.

1 What is Len wearing?

2 How can you tell that Len is a tidy person?

3 Why could he clear the weeds and rubbish quickly?

4 What does this sentence tell you about Len?

Len worked steadily as he was determined to finish the hole before he went in for lunch.

5 How do you know that Len:

a liked working in the garden? b was kind and helpful?

C How is the story written? Discuss your answers.

1 Look at the verbs in the story, for example:

was *decided* *were* *hanging*

What tenses are they written in?

2 Where is the story set?

3 Who are the main characters?

4 How many paragraphs are there in the story?

5 Say briefly what each paragraph is about.

Let's learn

Proper nouns

Proper nouns have capital letters.
The names of characters are proper nouns.
Len **G**race **M**rs **B**rown

Sometimes we want to let readers know when a story happened.
Days of the week and **months** of the year are proper nouns.
Saturday **J**une

Sometimes we want to let readers know where characters live.
The names of **streets**, **towns**, **cities** and **countries** are proper nouns.
Bank **S**treet **L**ondon **S**cotland

A Write these proper nouns with capital letters.

1 tuesday ______ 2 green street ______

3 mira ______ 4 china ______

5 amman ______ 6 august ______

B Write:

1 your name ___

2 the name of the street where you live ___

3 the name of the town/city where you live ___

4 the country you live in ___

Pronouns

We can use **pronouns** instead of nouns so we do not have to repeat a character's name over and over again.

Len decided to work in the garden. **He** dressed quickly.

noun (Len) pronoun (He)

These are pronouns: **I** **you** **he** **she** **it** **we** **they**

A Write the pronoun you could use instead of each underlined noun.

1 <u>Len</u> was digging in the garden. ___

2 <u>Grace</u> brought him a cup of tea. ___

3 <u>Len and Grace</u> talked about the pond. ___

4 <u>Mrs Brown</u> asked for help. ___

5 <u>The cat</u> was stuck in the tree. ___

Past tenses

Stories are usually written in **past tenses**.

Verbs have different **tenses**: **past**, **present** and **future**.

Past tenses:	Len **stepped**.	Len **was stepping**.
	Len **got**…	Len **was getting**…

A Find and copy six more examples of past tenses in the story.

1 ___ 2 ___

3 ___ 4 ___

5 ___ 6 ___

B Write these present tense sentences in the past tense.

1 Grace is marking Year 4's stories.

____

2 Len takes his rake from the shed.

____

3 He is clearing the weeds and the rubbish.

____

4 Len drinks his tea.

____

5 The cat runs up the tree.

____

Adjectives

Adjectives describe nouns.

We use adjectives so readers can imagine what characters and other things in stories look like.

patched jeans **large** rake **heavy** wheelbarrow

A Find and copy adjectives in the story that describe:

1 Len's T-shirt ______________________________

2 Len's boots ______________________________

3 Len's hair ______________________________

4 the weeds ______________________________

5 the tea ______________________________

B Think of two adjectives that you could use to describe:

1 the shed ______________ ______________

2 the gate ______________ ______________

3 the tree ______________ ______________

4 the ladder ______________ ______________

5 the cat ______________ ______________

Adverbs

Adverbs tell us more about verbs.

We use adverbs in stories to show how something is done.

Len dressed **quickly**.
How did Len dress? **quickly**

The tools were hanging **neatly**.
How were the tools hanging? **neatly**

Top Tip

Adverbs add to verbs.

A Find and copy the adverbs in the story that show how:

1 Len was humming ______________________

2 Len pushed the wheelbarrow ______________________

3 Len jumped out of the hole ______________________

4 Mrs Brown asked for Len's help ______________________

5 Grace came out of the house ______________________

B Think of an adverb for how:

1 Len cleared the weeds ______________________

2 Grace carried the tea ______________________

3 Len drank his tea ______________________

4 Mrs Brown cried, "Len!" ______________________

5 The dog was barking ______________________

Creating characters

A very important part of any story is the **characters**.

You need to think about:

- what your characters look like – **physical appearance**
- what sort of people they are – **personality**.

You also need to think about how you want your readers to **feel** about your characters. Do you want your readers to:

- like them?
- dislike them?

How readers feel about your characters depends on:

- how you **describe** them
- how they **behave**.

A Physical appearance

1 What do we know about what Len looks like?

- We know he has *black, curly hair.*
- We know he is *fit and strong.*

2 Talk about others things the writer could have described.

- the colour of Len's eyes: blue brown green grey
- Len's size: tall / short thin / overweight

3 What do we know about how Len is dressed?

- We know that his clothes are *patched* and *old.*
- We know that his boots are *muddy.*

4 Talk about how you would describe:

- Len's gardening gloves: dirty / clean new / worn
- Len's baseball cap: colour? logo?

5 Talk about how you think Len would be dressed when he was going to work as a firefighter.

- Would he wear a uniform?
- What would it look like?
- Would he be smart or scruffy?

B Personality

1 What do we know about Len's personality?

- We know Len is hardworking.

  Len worked steadily as he was determined to finish the hole before he went in for lunch.

- We know that he likes things neat and tidy.

  He kept his gardening tools there. They were hanging neatly on hooks or lined up on the workbench.

- We know that he is kind and helpful.

  "Of course I'll help. Don't worry. I'll soon have her down."

2 Talk about how you think Len behaves when he is working as a firefighter. Which of these words and phrases do you think best describes Len's personality?

Word box

not afraid of hard work	lazy	selfish
brave	cowardly	kind
messy	thinks about other people	cruel

3 Add some words and phrases of your own to describe Len's personality.

______________________ ______________________

______________________ ______________________

______________________ ______________________

______________________ ______________________

4 If you met Len, do you think you would like him? Why, or why not?

____

____

____

____

____

____

____

Let's practise

The only things we know about Grace from the story extract are:

- she brings her husband a cup of tea
- she is a teacher
- she is marking Year 4's stories.

You are going to write a character description of Grace as she sits at the kitchen table marking Year 4's stories. Use your imagination!

A Planning

Use the questions below to help you.

1 Physical appearance

- Is Grace:
  - tall or short? ______________________
  - overweight or thin? ______________________
- What is her hair like?
  - What colour is it? ______________________
  - Is it straight or curly? ______________________
  - Is it long or short? ______________________
- What are her eyes like?
  - What colour are they? ______________________
  - Are they large or small? ______________________
- How is Grace dressed?

List the clothes she is wearing. Write adjectives to describe her clothes.

Grace is wearing:

Item of clothing	Adjectives
______________	______________________
______________	______________________
______________	______________________

- Add any other details of her physical appearance you want to describe.

____

____

2 Personality

- Does Grace read the children's work carefully or hurriedly? ______________
- Is her marking neat or scruffy? ______________
- Are the books on the table neat or in a mess? ______________
- Does she write helpful comments or just put ticks and crosses? ______________
- Does she sigh or smile as she works? ______________
- What does she say to herself as she works? ______________
- Does she look bad tempered, energetic, tired, or something else? ______________

B Writing

Now use your notes to write your description of Grace as she sits at the kitchen table marking Year 4's stories.

Writer's Toolbox

Have you:

- used capital letters for **proper nouns**?
- used **pronouns**?
- written in **past tenses**?
- used **adjectives** to describe Grace's physical appearance?
- used **adverbs** to show how she does things?
- described Grace's **personality**?

Edit and proofread

Correct any mistakes in: spelling punctuation grammar

Write your neat copy.

Let's write

In the story extract, the only things we know about Mrs Brown are:

- she lives on the same street as Len and Grace
- she has a cat
- she is upset
- she is polite.

You are going to write a character description of Mrs Brown. There are very few clues in the story extract so you can use your imagination. Try to make her a very different character from Grace.

A Planning

Use the questions below to help you.

1 Physical appearance

- Is Mrs Brown:
  - tall or short? ______________________________
  - overweight or thin? ______________________________
- What is her hair like?
  - What colour is it? ______________________________
  - Is it straight or curly? ______________________________
  - Is it long or short? ______________________________
- What are her eyes like?
  - What colour are they? ______________________________
  - Are they large or small? ______________________________
- How is Mrs Brown dressed?
  - List the clothes she is wearing.
  - Write adjectives to describe the clothes.

  Mrs Brown is wearing:

Item of clothing	Adjectives
______________	______________________________
______________	______________________________
______________	______________________________

- Add any other details of her physical appearance you want to describe.

____

____

2 Personality

- Is Mrs Brown kind-hearted or cruel? ______________________
- Is she rude or polite? ______________________
- Is she helpful or selfish? ______________________
- Is she shy or bossy? ______________________
- Is she happy or miserable? ______________________
- Add any other details of her personality you want to describe.

____

____

____

B Writing

Now use your notes to write your character description.

Writer's Toolbox

Have you:

- used capital letters for **proper nouns**?
- used **pronouns**?
- written in **past tenses**?
- used **adjectives** to describe physical appearance?
- used **adverbs** to show how she does things?
- described Mrs Brown's **personality**?

Edit and proofread

Correct any mistakes in: spelling punctuation grammar

Write your neat copy.

3 Poetry: acrostics and haikus

Acrostic poems

Many types of **poem** describe what the poet sees. They paint a picture with words.

An **acrostic** is a form of poem where the first letter of each line spells a word.

Let's read

Read this acrostic poem.

Let's talk

A What is the poem about? Discuss your answers.

1 What time of day is the poem describing?

2 Where does the sun set?

3 What has *Gone*?

4 What *approaches*?

5 What word is spelled by the first letter of each line?

B How is an acrostic written? Discuss your answers.

1 Why do you think the poet had to think carefully about the first word in every line?

2 Is every line in the acrostic a complete sentence?

3 Find an example in the acrostic of a line that is:

a one word b a phrase c a sentence.

4 Find three examples of adjectives in the acrostic.

5 Does the acrostic rhyme?

Some poets use **rhyme** in their **acrostics**.

Let's read

Daylight

See the burning sun
Up high in the sky
Night has faded quickly
Stars have said goodbye
Happy birds now sing
In the morning light
Now the dark is over
Earth is warm and bright.

Let's talk

A What is the poem about? Discuss your answers.

1 What time of day is the poem describing?

2 What has *faded quickly*?

3 What has said *goodbye*?

4 What word is spelled by the first letter of each line?

B How is an acrostic written? Discuss your answers.

1 Is every line in the acrostic a complete sentence?

2 Find an example in the acrostic of a line that is:

a a phrase b a sentence.

3 Find three examples of adjectives in the acrostic.

4 Which words rhyme in the acrostic?

Let's learn

Adjectives

Adjectives describe nouns.

Adjectives help readers to imagine what the poet is describing.

black **inky** **warm** and **bright**

A Make a list of adjectives that you could use to describe:

1 the night

______ ______
______ ______
______ ______

2 daylight

______ ______
______ ______
______ ______

Rhyme

Rhyming words have the same sound.

light ***bright***

Some rhyming words are **spelled differently** but sound the same.

sky ***goodbye***

A Add more rhymes for these words.

1 light ______ ______ ______

2 sky ______ ______ ______

-ing adjectives

Some words ending in *-ing* can be used as **adjectives**.

*See the **burning** sun.*

A Add *-ing* to each word.

1 shine ______________ 2 frighten ______________

3 interest ______________ 4 surprise ______________

5 amaze ______________ 6 warm ______________

7 darken ______________ 8 boil ______________

B Use each of your *-ing* adjectives with a suitable noun.

1 ______________ 2 ______________

3 ______________ 4 ______________

5 ______________ 6 ______________

7 ______________ 8 ______________

Position of adjectives

Adjectives can come **before a noun**.

__happy__ birds

Adjectives can come **after a noun**.

Earth is __warm__ and __bright__.

A Make each sentence into a phrase so that the adjective comes before the noun.

1 The sky is black. ______________

2 The birds are screeching. ______________

3 The sun is hot. ______________

4 The day is warm. ______________

5 The night is cold. ______________

Let's practise

You are going to write an acrostic poem, using the words A SUNNY DAY.

A Planning

1 Make a list of the **adjectives** you could use to describe a sunny day.

_______________ _______________ _______________

_______________ _______________ _______________

2 Think about what you are going to describe. Tick one of these.

Is it a sunny day

on the beach? ☐ in a park? ☐ at school? ☐

3 Make a list of things people might do on a sunny day.

_______________ _______________ _______________

_______________ _______________ _______________

_______________ _______________ _______________

4 These are some of the letters that will begin the lines in your poem.

Here are some words you could use.

Add some more words to each list.

A above after all although and any a

_______________ _______________ _______________

S said sat shall she should so

_______________ _______________ _______________

U under unless up

_______________ _______________ _______________

N never new no not now

_______________ _______________ _______________

Y yes yet you your

_______________ _______________ _______________

D did didn't do don't

_______________ _______________ _______________

B Writing

Now use your notes to write your acrostic poem.

Remember! Not every line has to be a complete sentence.

You can use single words and phrases.

A ______________________________

S ______________________________

U ______________________________

N ______________________________

N ______________________________

Y ______________________________

D ______________________________

A ______________________________

Y ______________________________

Writer's Toolbox

Have you:

- started each line with the **correct letter**?
- used **interesting adjectives**?
- used **sentences**, **phrases** and **single words**?

Edit and proofread

Correct any mistakes in: spelling punctuation grammar

Write your neat copy.

Let's write

You are going to write an acrostic poem using the words THE MOON.

A Planning

Think about:

- adjectives you can use to describe the Moon
- where you are when you look at the Moon.

B Writing

- Write **THE MOON** with each letter on a new line.
- Write your **first draft**.
- Use the **Writer's Toolbox on page 37**.
- Find and correct any mistakes in **spelling**, **punctuation** and **grammar**.
- Write your **neat copy**.

Haikus

Many types of **poem** describe what the poet sees. Poets paint a picture with words!

A **haiku** is a form of poem that:
- has three lines
- describes something you see in one moment of time.

Let's read

Read this haiku.

The Sun

Orange glowing ball
Beating down upon the Earth
Parched and dusty ground.

Let's talk

A What is the haiku about? Discuss your answers.

1 What adjectives describe the sun?

2 What adjectives describe the ground?

3 What picture forms in your mind as you read the haiku?

Let's read

Read this haiku.

The Moon

Crescent in the sky
Against the inky black night
Glowing silver gem.

Let's talk

A What is the haiku about? Discuss your answers.

1 What shape is the Moon?

2 What adjectives describe the Moon?

3 What is the colour of the night?

4 What picture forms in your mind as you read the haiku?

B How is a haiku written? Discuss your answers.

1 How many lines does a haiku have?

2 How many syllables are there in:

a the first line? b the second line? c the third line?

Let's learn

Syllables

A **syllable** is a unit of speech.

Some words are made up of **one** syllable, for example:

sun **moon**

Some words have **two** syllables, for example:

glowing – glow-ing **inky – in-ky**

Words can have **lots** of syllables, for example:

approaches **ap-proa-ches**

A Split these words into their syllables.

	1st syllable	2nd syllable	3rd syllable
1 ground			
2 dusty			
3 adjective			
4 western			
5 imagine			

Let's practise

You are going to write a **haiku** about this photograph.

A Planning

1 Begin by listing three things you can see in the photograph. Include the colours and other adjectives.

a ______________________

b ______________________

c ______________________

2 Write a short sentence about the thing you have listed in **a**.

____

3 Write a short sentence about the thing you have listed in **b**.

____

4 Write a short sentence about the thing you have listed in **c**.

____

B Writing

1 Read your first sentence. Reduce it to five syllables.

____

2 Read your second sentence. Reduce it to seven syllables.

____

3 Read your third sentence. Reduce it to five syllables.

____

4 Give your haiku a title. _______________

Writer's Toolbox

Make sure you have:

- only **three lines** in your haiku
- **five syllables** in the first line
- **seven syllables** in the second line
- **five syllables** in the last line
- given your haiku a **title**.

Edit and proofread

Correct any mistakes in: spelling punctuation grammar

Write your neat copy.

Let's write

You are going to write a haiku about this photograph.

A Planning

- Look at the photograph carefully.
- List three things you can see in it.

B Writing

- Write **three sentences** about what you can see.
- Reduce the sentences to **five**, **seven** and **five** syllable lines.
- Give your haiku a **title**.
- Use the **Writer's Toolbox**, above.
- **Edit and proofread**, correcting any mistakes in **spelling**, **punctuation** and **grammar**.

4 Factual writing: reports

When you find out the **facts** about a subject and put them in a piece of writing, you produce a **factual report**.

Let's read

Read this report on the skyscraper the Burj Khalifa.

The Burj Khalifa

The Burj Khalifa is the tallest building in the world, to date. It is located in Dubai, in the United Arab Emirates. Building work began on 6th January 2004. It was opened with a magnificent ceremony on 4th January 2010.

The Burj Khalifa is made of concrete, steel, aluminium and glass. It took more than 110,000 tons of concrete to build, which weighs about as much as 100,000 elephants, and 55,000 tons of steel. It took 22 million working hours to build!

There are 163 floors in the Burj Khalifa. It is 829.8 metres (2723 feet) to the very tip of the building. There are 57 lifts, which travel at 10 metres per second, and 8 escalators. It has 304 hotel rooms, 900 apartments and 2957 parking spaces.

Outside the building is a very special feature called the Dubai Fountain. It is 270 metres (900 feet) long and has 6600 lights. The water shoots 150 metres (500 feet) into the air, making amazing shapes and patterns. The water twists and turns as if it is dancing to the classical, modern and Arabian music that plays during the performance.

Visitors to the Burj Khalifa can go up to the two observation decks to see spectacular views of the city. The deck on the 124th floor is 452 metres (1483 feet) high. Even higher is the deck on the 148th floor where visitors can look down from a height of 555 metres (1821 feet). These observation decks have floor to ceiling glass walls so visitors can walk round and see the whole of Dubai and the surrounding desert. There is also a restaurant called *At.mosphere*, which is on the 122nd floor. Visitors can enjoy a meal while taking in the view.

Let's talk

A What is the report about? Discuss your answers.

1 Where is the Burj Khalifa?

2 What is it made of?

3 How tall is it?

4 When did building begin?

5 When did it open?

B Looking at the facts. Discuss your answers.

1 How many tons of concrete did it take to build the Burj Khalifa?

2 How many tons of steel did it take to build?

3 What are there:

a 163 of? b 57 of? c 2957 of?

4 What is 270 metres long and has 6600 lights?

5 What is on the 122nd floor?

C How is the report written? Discuss your answers.

1 Why do you think the writer begins the report with this sentence?

The Burj Khalifa is the tallest building in the world, to date.

2 Some of the report is written using past tense verbs, for example:

began *was opened* *took*

Why are these verbs in the past tense?

3 Some of the report is written using present tense verbs, for example:

are *shoots* *is dancing*

Why are these verbs in the present tense?

4 How many paragraphs are there in the report?

5 Say briefly what each paragraph is about.

6 What illustrations has the writer used in the report?

7 Do you find them useful? Why, or why not?

Let's learn

Verb tenses

Reports can be written in **past** and **present tenses**.

If something in the report has happened in the **past**, the writer uses **past tense verbs**.
It ***was opened*** *with a magnificent ceremony on 4th January 2010.*

If something in the report is still happening, the writer uses **present tense verbs**.
The water ***shoots*** *150 metres (500 feet) into the air,* ***making*** *amazing shapes and patterns.*

Top Tip

Tense means **time**.

A Underline the past tense verbs in these sentences. Write each sentence in the present tense.

1 I visited the Burj Khalifa.

____

2 She liked the fountain.

____

3 The escalator travelled at 10 metres per second.

____

B Underline the present tense verbs in these sentences. Write each sentence in the past tense.

1 I am reading about the Burj Khalifa.

____

2 We are looking at the view.

____

3 They play classical music.

____

C Use these verbs in sentences of your own.

1 was twisting _______________

____

2 are visiting _______________

____

How to write a report

When you write a report, you need to plan your work like this:

Step 1: **research**

Step 2: make **notes**

Step 3: **order** the notes

Step 4: write the **first draft**

Step 5: **proofread** and **edit**

Step 6: write the **final copy**

Step 7: give the report a **title**

Step 1: Research

- The first step is to find the information you need.
- You can use books, magazines and websites.

The writer of the report on the Burj Khalifa used these books.

The World's Tallest Building

The Burj Khalifa in Dubai, one of the United Arab Emirates, was opened on 4 January 2010. The amount of concrete in the building weighs as much as 100,000 elephants! Elevators travelling at 10 metres per second take visitors to two observation decks. The first is on the 124th floor at a height of 452 metres (1483 feet). The second is on the 148th floor at a height of 555 metres (1821 feet). Each observation deck has floor to ceiling glass walls so people can see the spectacular views on all sides.

The Burj Khalifa

The Burj Khalifa is 829.8 metres (2723 feet) tall.

Building began on this desert skyscraper on 6 January 2004 and took 22 million man hours to complete.

Outside the building is the Dubai Fountain. Water from the 270-metre (900 feet) long fountain shoots 150 metres (500 feet) into the air. It is lit by 6600 lights. The water dances to the music, which is a mixture of classical, modern and Arabian.

Skyscraper in the Desert

This amazing building is made of concrete, steel, aluminium and glass. 110,000 tons of concrete and 55000 tons of steel went into the building. Inside, it has 163 floors, 57 elevators and 8 escalators. There are 304 hotel rooms, 900 apartments and 2957 parking spaces. There is also a restaurant on the 122nd floor called *At.mosphere.*

Step 2: Make notes

- The second step is to make notes of the information you find.
- Notes do not have to be written in complete sentences.
- Do **not** copy whole sentences or paragraphs.
- Use words and short phrases.

Here are the notes the writer of the report made.

The World's Tallest Building

Dubai – United Arab Emirates

opened – 4 January 2010

concrete – weighs as much as 100,000 elephants

observation decks – floor to ceiling glass walls

- 124th floor – 453 m (1483 ft)
- 148th floor – 555 m (1821 ft)

elevators travel at 10 m per second

The Burj Khalifa

829.8 m high (2723 ft)

building began 6 January 2004

22 million man hours to build

Dubai Fountain:

- 270 m long (900 ft)
- water shoots 150 m high (500 ft)
- 6600 lights
- water 'dances' to music
- classical, modern, Arabian

Skyscraper in the Desert

made of concrete, steel, aluminium and glass

110,000 tons of concrete

55,000 tons of steel

163 floors

57 elevators

8 escalators

304 hotel rooms

900 apartments

2957 parking spaces

122nd floor – *At.mosphere* restaurant

Step 3: Order your notes

The writer looked at her notes and decided she could group the information into five paragraphs for the report.

Paragraph 1: where the Burj Khalifa is and when it was built

She looked for information in her notes and highlighted the notes in yellow.

Dubai – United Arab Emirates

opened – 4 January 2010

building began 6 January 2004

Paragraph 2: what the Burj Khalifa is made of

She looked for information in her notes and highlighted the notes in green.

made of concrete, steel, aluminium and glass

110,000 tons of concrete

concrete – weighs as much as 100,000 elephants

55,000 tons of steel

22 million man hours to build

Paragraph 3: what is in the Burj Khalifa

She looked for information in her notes and highlighted the notes in blue.

829.8 m high (2723 ft)

163 floors

57 elevators – travel at 10 m per second

8 escalators

304 hotel rooms

900 apartments

2957 parking spaces

Paragraph 4: The Dubai Fountain

She looked for information in her notes and highlighted the notes in purple.

Dubai Fountain:

– 270 m long (900 ft)

– water shoots 150 m high (500 ft)

– 6600 lights

– water 'dances' to music

– classical, modern, Arabian

Paragraph 5: what visitors can see and do

She looked for information in her notes and highlighted the notes in grey.

observation decks – floor to ceiling glass walls

124th floor – 453 m (1483 ft)

148th floor – 555 m (1821 ft)

122nd floor – *At.mosphere* restaurant

The writer finished her report by following these steps:

Step 4: She wrote her **first draft** from her notes. She made sure the first sentence made it clear what the report was about.

Step 5: She read through her first draft to **proofread** it. She **corrected mistakes** in spelling, punctuation and grammar.

Step 6: She wrote the **final copy**.

Step 7: She gave her report a **title** – *The Burj Khalifa.*

Let's practise

You are going to write a report on the Petronas Twin Towers in Malaysia.

A Planning

Step 1: Research

Here are three books that give information about the Petronas Twin Towers.

The Twin Towers

The Petronas Twin Towers are in Malaysia. Between 1998 and 2004 they were the tallest buildings in the world. Building began in March 1993 and was completed in 1998. Their main use is as offices. A skybridge connects the two towers on the 41st and 42nd floors.

The towers are surrounded by nearly 70 acres of parkland.

The Tallest Towers in the World

In the city of Kuala Lumpur can be seen the tallest twin towers in the world. The Petronas Twin Towers were opened on 28 August 1999. They rise to 452 metres (1483 feet) high. Each tower has 29 elevators. The skybridge, weighing 750 tons, is 170 metres (558 feet) above ground. The ground floor has a huge shopping centre. Outside is a fountain with lightshow and a children's playground.

Towers in the Sky

The Petronas Twin Towers are made of concrete, glass and steel. They are connected by a skybridge that is 58.4 metres (192 feet) long. Inside there are offices, shops, an art gallery, a concert hall and an aquarium. Outside there is a public park with jogging and walking paths and wading pools.

Step 2: Make notes

Write the important facts from each book in note form.

The Twin Towers

The Tallest Towers in the World

Towers in the Sky

Step 3: Order your notes

Put the notes in the correct paragraph.

Paragraph 1: What are the Twin Towers? Where are the Twin Towers?

Paragraph 2: How tall are they? When were they built? What are they made of?

Paragraph 3: Inside the Twin Towers

Paragraph 4: The skybridge

Paragraph 5: Around the Twin Towers

B Writing

Step 4: Write your **first draft** using your notes. Make sure your first sentence makes it clear what the report is about.

Step 5: Read through your first draft. **Proofread** and **correct any mistakes** in spelling, punctuation and grammar. Check your verb tenses.

Step 6: Write your **final copy**.

Step 7: Give your report a **title**. ______________________________

Let's write

You are going to write a report on a building in your area.

A Planning

Choose the building you are going to write about.

____

Step 1: Do your **research**. Find books, magazines and websites that will give you information about your building.

Step 2: Make **notes** of the important information you find out about your building. Remember!

- Notes do not have to be written in complete sentences.
- Do **not** copy whole sentences or paragraphs.
- Use words and short phrases.

Step 3: How many paragraphs will you have in your report? **Order your notes** into paragraphs.

B Writing

Step 4: Write your **first draft** using your notes.

Step 5: Read through your first draft. **Proofread** and **correct any mistakes** in spelling, punctuation and grammar. Check your verb tenses.

Step 6: Write your **final copy**.

Step 7: Give your report a **title**. ______________________________

5 Narrative writing: dialogue in stories

Dialogue is when we write what characters actually say.

We write their **conversation**.

Let's read

Read this extract from a story called *Schooldays*.

Tom, Sam and Abi are triplets. They are in Class 4 at Fallow Primary School.

Schooldays

In this extract, Class 4 has been learning about Neil Armstrong.

He was an astronaut and the first person to walk on the Moon.

For homework, they have to write about what they want to be when they grow up. On the way home, Tom, Sam and Abi talk about what they are going to write.

"I've decided I'm going to be an astronaut," said Abi.

"Why would you want to do that?" asked Tom.

"It's exciting and dangerous!" said Abi.

"What are you going to write about, Sam?" asked Tom.

Sam thought for a moment and said, "I don't know. I wouldn't want to go into space. It's too scary!"

"I think I'd like to be a doctor," said Tom.

Abi pulled a face. "Ugh! All that blood!" she exclaimed. "Why would you want to be a doctor?"

Tom replied, "Well, you can help people. I might find a cure for some disease and be famous. That's better than standing on the Moon."

"What about you, Sam?" asked Abi. "What do you want to be when you grow up?"

"It's a secret," said Sam.

"That's not fair! We've told you what we want to be. You've got to tell us!" exclaimed Abi.

"You'll find out tomorrow," whispered Sam mysteriously, "when we read our homework to the class."

Let's talk

A What is the extract about? Discuss your answers.

1 Who are the three characters having a conversation?

2 What are they talking about?

3 Who wants to be an astronaut?

4 Who wants to be a doctor?

5 What do you think Sam might want to be?

6 What do you want to be when you grow up? Why?

B Looking at dialogue. Discuss your answers.

1 In the extract, find an example of:

a something Sam says

b something Tom says

c something Abi says

2 Find an example where:

a the speaker's name comes *before* the spoken words

b the speaker's name comes *after* the spoken words.

C Words instead of *said*

1 Find three examples of words the writer has used instead of *said*. Discuss your answers.

Let's learn

Dialogue

A reader knows who is speaking because the writer:

- uses **speech marks** around the spoken words
- names the **speaker**
- uses a **comma** between the spoken words and the non-spoken words
- uses a **capital letter** for the first word spoken.

A Add the missing speech marks.

1 Neil Armstrong was the first person to land on the Moon, said the teacher.

2 Tom said, Doctors help people.

3 I want to be an astronaut, said Abi.

4 You'll find out tomorrow, whispered Sam.

You need to think carefully about what your characters say.

If a character asks a **question**, use a **question mark**.
*"Why would you want to do that**?**" asked Tom.*

If a character makes an **exclamation**, use an **exclamation mark**.
*"Ugh! All that blood**!**" she exclaimed.*

B Add the missing punctuation.

1 I want to be a doctor said Tom

2 Who is Neil Armstrong asked Sam

3 That's scary exclaimed Sam

4 What do you want to be asked Abi

Top Tip

If the speech is not a question or an exclamation, use a comma.

Paragraphing

When we write dialogue, we start a **new paragraph** when a different person speaks.

We start a new paragraph by leaving a space between the margin and the first word.

Sam thought for a moment and said, "I don't know. I wouldn't want to go into space. It's too scary!"

"I think I'd like to be a doctor," said Tom.

A Copy this dialogue and set it out correctly.

"Do you think Neil Armstrong was scared when he went into space?" asked Tom. Sam said, "I know I would be." "I don't think he was scared. I think he was very brave," said Abi.

______

______

______

______

______

Contractions

When we speak we often use short forms of words.

We say:

I'm for **I am** ***he's*** for **he is** ***let's*** for **let us**

These are called **contractions**.

They have an **apostrophe** for the missing letters.

Use contractions when you write dialogue.

A Find and write three examples of contractions in the extract from *Schooldays*.

1 ______

2 ______

3 ______

B **Write these as contractions.**

1 we are ______________________
2 they will ______________________
3 cannot ______________________
4 was not ______________________
5 is not ______________________
6 I will ______________________
7 will not ______________________
8 could not ______________________

C **Write these contractions in full.**

1 it's ______________________
2 shouldn't ______________________
3 let's ______________________
4 haven't ______________________
5 didn't ______________________
6 they've ______________________
7 aren't ______________________
8 I'm ______________________

Synonyms for *said*

A **synonym** is a word that means the same, or nearly the same, as another word.

When we write dialogue, we can use more interesting words than **said**.

In *Schooldays*:

Tom ***asked***… Abi ***exclaimed***… Sam ***whispered***…

A **Write these synonyms for said in the correct box.**

muttered yelled shouted

mumbled cried whispered

something said **loudly**	something said **quietly**
______________________	______________________
______________________	______________________
______________________	______________________

B Choose a synonym from the box in A to complete each sentence.

1 "Shhh," ______________________________ Tom.

2 "Help!" ______________________________ Abi.

3 "That hurts!" ______________________________ Sam.

4 "I'll tell you a secret," ______________________________ Abi.

Split direct speech

Sometimes the words a character says are **split** by the character's name or pronoun.

The character's name or pronoun can come **in the middle of one sentence**:

"You'll find out tomorrow," whispered ***Sam*** *mysteriously, "when we read our homework to the class."*

The character's name or pronoun can come **between two sentences**:

"Ugh! All that blood!" ***she*** *exclaimed. "Why would you want to be a doctor?"*

A Punctuate these direct speech sentences.

1 I've decided said Abi to be an astronaut

2 I wouldn't want to go into space said Sam It's too scary

3 I might find a cure for some disease said Sam I might be famous

4 Sam won't tell us what he wants to be said Abi because he doesn't know

B Write one sentence about what you want to be when you grow up.

Split what you say using the words *I said*.

____

____

C Write two sentences about what you want to be when you grow up.

Split what you say using the words *I said*.

____

____

Let's practise

This is the next part of the story:

Tom, Abi and Sam were walking to school the next morning.

Abi had done her homework. She had written about being an astronaut.

Tom had done his homework. He had written about being a doctor.

Tom and Abi wanted to know what Sam had written about.

You are going to write the conversation the triplets have on their way to school.

A Planning

Use the questions below to help you plan their conversation.

Write the children's questions and answers.

1 Abi asked Sam what he had written about. What do you think Abi said?

____

____

2 Sam wouldn't tell her. What do you think Sam said?

____

____

3 Tom tried to make Sam tell him. What do you think Tom said?

____

____

4 Sam said they could try to guess. What do you think Sam said?

____

____

5 Abi had a guess. What do you think Abi said?

____

____

6 Sam told her she was wrong. What do you think Sam said?

7 Tom had a guess. What do you think Tom said?

8 Sam told Tom he was wrong. He told Abi and Tom what he wrote about. What do you think Sam said?

B Writing

Now write the children's conversation.

Remember to:

- use a new **paragraph** when a different person speaks
- name the **speaker**.

Writer's Toolbox

Have you:

- put **speech marks** around the spoken words?
- used a **capital letter** for the first word spoken?
- used an **exclamation mark** for an exclamation?
- used **contractions**?
- used a **comma** between the spoken and non-spoken words?
- used **synonyms** instead of said?
- used **split direct speech**?
- used a **question mark** for a question?

Edit and proofread

Correct any mistakes in: spelling punctuation grammar

Write your neat copy.

Let's write

Sam and Tom are going to play football in their PE lesson. They talk about football as they are putting on their football boots.

Tom doesn't like football.

Sam really loves football.

You are going to write their conversation.

A Planning

Here are some things to think about as you plan their conversation.

1 These are some words the children could use to talk about football.

Which words would Tom use?

Which words would Sam use?

Write them in the correct list.

Word box

wonderful	horrible	boring	exciting
silly	great	dull	brilliant

Sam's list

____

____

____

____

Tom's list

____

____

____

____

2 Sam is putting on his football boots. He is very excited.

What does he say?

____

____

____

3 Tom is holding his boots. He is not looking forward to the game.

What does he say?

____

____

____

4 Sam asks Tom why he doesn't like football.

What does Sam say?

____

____

____

5 Tom explains why he doesn't like football.

What does he say?

____

____

____

6 Tom asks Sam why he likes football.

What does Tom say?

____

____

____

7 Sam explains why he likes football.

What does he say?

____

____

____

8 Here are some words you could use instead of said.

Word box

mumbled	shouted	laughed
shrieked	asked	grumbled

Add some more **synonyms for said** to the list.

____________________ ____________________

____________________ ____________________

____________________ ____________________

____________________ ____________________

____________________ ____________________

____________________ ____________________

B Writing

Now write your first draft.

Writer's Toolbox

Have you:

• put **speech marks** around the spoken words?	
• used a **comma** between the spoken and non-spoken words?	"I like these boots**,**" said Sam.
• used a **capital letter** for the first word spoken?	
• used a **question mark** for a question?	"Where are your boots**?**" asked Sam
• used an **exclamation mark** for an exclamation?	"I've lost them**!**" said Tom.
• used **synonyms** instead of *said*?	"You'll miss the game!" **shrieked** Sam.
• used **contractions**?	"You **can't** play without boots," said Sam.
• used **split** direct speech?	"**I put my boots here**," said Tom, "**and now they're gone**!"
• begun a **new paragraph** when a different person speaks?	"You'll miss the game!" shrieked Sam. "You can't play without boots!" "I put my boots here," said Tom, "and now they're gone!"

Edit and proofread

Correct any mistakes in: spelling punctuation grammar

Write your neat copy.

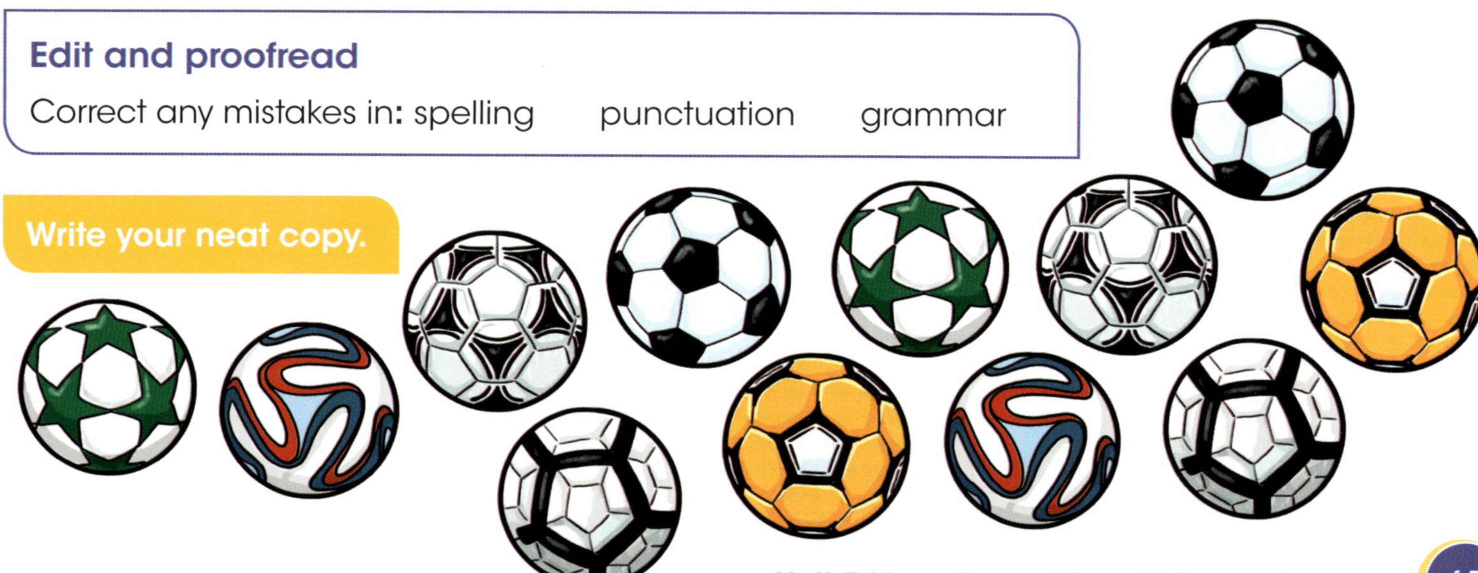

6 Instructional writing: recipes

A recipe is a set of **instructions** showing you how to make something to eat.

Let's read

Read this recipe for fishcakes.

Easy Thai Fishcakes

Ingredients

400 g boneless pollock fillets

1 tbsp Thai red curry paste

2 tsp fish sauce

zest of 1 lime

1 egg white

0.5 g lemongrass

1 tbsp coriander leaves

50 g green beans

1 red chilli pepper

2 tbsp sesame seeds

sunflower oil

Method

1 Chop the pollock fillets into small pieces.
2 Chop the lemongrass into small pieces.
3 Slice the green beans thinly.
4 Remove the seeds from the chilli.
5 Chop the chilli into small pieces.
6 Put the pollock, curry paste, fish sauce, lime zest, egg white, lemongrass and coriander into a food processor.
7 Whizz to a smooth paste.

8 Put the paste into a bowl.

9 Add the beans and chilli.

10 Mix together thoroughly.

11 Shape the mixture into 15 small fishcakes.

12 Sprinkle both sides with sesame seeds.

13 Arrange the fishcakes on a baking tray.

14 Chill for an hour in the fridge.

15 Heat the oil gently in a frying pan.

16 Fry the fishcakes quickly, a few at a time, until golden brown.

Let's talk

A What does the recipe tell you? Discuss your answers.

1 What will you make if you follow these instructions?

2 How many instructions are there?

3 What do you need:

a 400g of? b 0.5g of? c 50g of?

4 What must you remove the seeds from?

5 How many fishcakes does the recipe make?

B Think about recipes. Discuss your answers.

1 Where can you find recipes?

2 Do you think these instructions are easy to follow? Why? Why not?

3 Would you like to eat these fishcakes? Why? Why not?

4 Have you ever made anything following a recipe?

a What did you make? b What would you like to make?

C How is a recipe written? Discuss your answers.

1 Why do you think the instructions are numbered?

2 Are the sentences:

a short and simple? b long and complicated?

3 Find the verb in each instruction.

4 Find the two subheadings in the recipe.

a What information does the first subheading give you?

b What information does the second subheading give you?

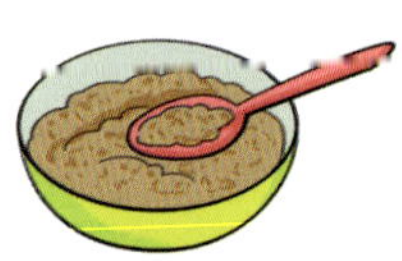

Let's learn

Headings and subheadings

Always begin your **instructions** with a **clear heading**.
This tells the reader what the instructions are for.

Easy Thai Fishcakes

Subheadings in instructions usually tell the reader:

1. The things they need to follow the instructions:

   Ingredients

2. The order in which to do things:

   Method

A Write these pieces of information under the correct heading.

2 tbsp of curry paste

Separate the egg white and egg yolk.

Take the skin off the fish.

3 coriander leaves

1 lime

Spoon in the fish sauce.

Ingredients

____

____

____

Method

____

____

____

Imperative verbs

Instructions use **imperative verbs.**
Imperative verbs are 'bossy' verbs.
They tell you what you must do.

Slice *the green beans.* ***Whizz*** *to a smooth paste.*

A Rewrite these sentences, beginning each one with an imperative verb.

The first one is done for you.

1 I have to chop the fish. Chop the fish.

2 I remove the seeds from the chilli pepper.

____

3 We use sunflower oil to fry the fishcakes.

____

Adverbs

Adverbs tell us more about verbs.
We use adverbs in instructions to show how something is done.

Slice the green beans **thinly**.

How do we slice the green beans? **thinly**

A Find and copy the adverbs in the instructions that show how:

1 to mix _______________

2 to heat the oil _______________

3 to fry the fishcakes _______________

B Think of an adverb for how you would:

1 remove the seeds from the chilli _______________

2 arrange the fishcakes on the tray _______________

Sentences

Instructions need to be **short** and **simple** so that readers can easily follow them.

Instructions mainly use **short sentences**.

8 *Put the paste into a bowl.*

9 *Add the beans and chilli.*

10 *Mix together thoroughly.*

A Write this long sentence as three short sentences. Use imperative verbs.

> You must chop the pollock fillets into small pieces then chop the lemongrass and slice the beans.

Sentence 1: ______________________________

____

Sentence 2: ______________________________

____

Sentence 3: ______________________________

____

Precise language

If instructions have **measurements** or **amounts**, you must use **precise** language.

2 tsp of fish sauce NOT **some** fish sauce

Top Tip

Precise means **exact**.

A Tick the phrases that use precise language.

1 2 tbsp sesame seeds ☐ **2** a few eggs ☐

3 lots of curry paste ☐ **4** 2 red chillis ☐

5 zest of 1 lime ☐ **6** chill for a while ☐

The layout of recipes

You must think carefully about how instructions **look on the page**.

- Begin with the **list of ingredients**.

  Write them in the order in which they are used.

  Use a new line for each ingredient.

- Follow the ingredients with the **method**.

  Write and number the instructions in the correct order.

  Use a new line for each instruction.

Ingredients

400g boneless pollock fillets

1 tbsp Thai red curry paste

2 tsp fish sauce

Method

1. *Chop the pollock into small pieces.*
2. *Chop the lemongrass stalk into small pieces.*
3. *Slice the green beans thinly.*

A Find the seven different instructions in this paragraph.

Rewrite the instructions so that:

- **each one is on a new line.**
- **each instruction has a number.**

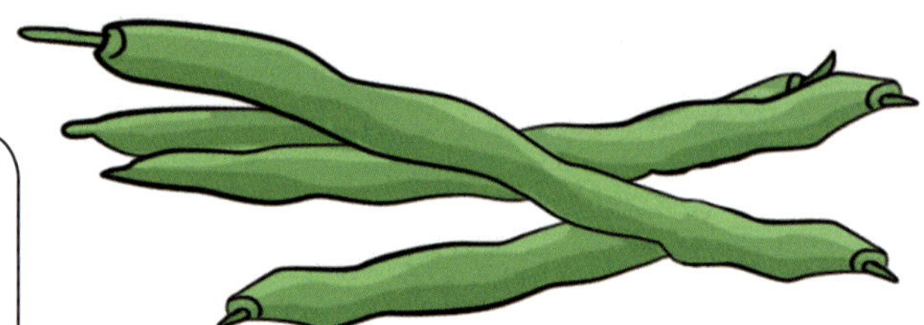

Cut off the ends of the green beans. Boil a pan of water. Put the green beans into the water. Turn down the heat. Cook for five minutes. Drain the beans. Add a knob of butter.

Let's practise

Jafar makes wonderful falafel.

His friend, Rabia, wanted the recipe.

He wrote it down for her, but it was not very clear.

Soak some chickpeas in water. You need 300 g of chickpeas. After you have soaked them for 12 hours, boil them in a pan. Drain them after they have boiled for 20 minutes. Get out the blender and blend the chickpeas to a smooth paste. Put some bulgur in with the paste before you blend it. You need 4 tbsp of bulgur and you should soak it in water for 1 hour before you use it. You have to add lots of other things to the paste. You have to put in 3 cloves of garlic and some salt. Before you put these in, crush the garlic and the salt. You need 1 tsp of salt. Add some flour and an egg. You need 3 tbsp of plain flour. You need some spices and herbs as well. You need 1 tsp of pepper, 3 tsp of coriander and 1 tsp of cumin. Don't forget to put in some red chilli — quarter of a tsp of chilli pepper will be enough. When you have added all these, mix them together thoroughly. Using your hands, carefully shape the paste into balls. It should make about 12. Put the balls on a baking tray and brush them gently with some oil. You can use vegetable oil or sunflower oil. Put them in the oven and bake them. They are ready when they look a golden brown colour. You should have the oven at 160 °C. If you have a gas oven, put it on at Gas mark 3. They should bake for about 15 minutes. I forgot to tell you to add 1 tbsp of tahini with the spices and herbs.

You are going to rewrite Jafar's instructions so they are clear and easy to follow.

A Planning

1 What will you call your recipe?

____

2 Read through Jafar's recipe and make a list of the ingredients.

- Remember to include all the amounts.
- Put each ingredient on a new line.

You should find 12 ingredients.

Ingredients

3 Now look at what to do with the ingredients.

Read Jafar's recipe again.

Make notes on everything he does with the ingredients – the method.

Method

B Writing

Now use your notes to write the recipe.

Writer's Toolbox

Have you:

- given your recipe a **title**?
- listed the ingredients in the **order** in which they are used?
- used **precise language**?
- put each ingredient on a **new line**?
- written the **method**:
  - in short, clear sentences?
  - in order?
- **numbered** the instructions?
- put each instruction on a **new line**?
- used **imperative verbs**?

Edit and proofread

Correct any mistakes in: spelling punctuation grammar

Write your neat copy.

Let's write

Here is another of Jafar's recipes. This is for panna cotta with figs and honey.

> This is delicious! You need a blender to whip together some cream and sugar. Use a quarter cup of cream and the same amount of sugar. Then you have to put in 1 cup of yogurt. This should be plain Greek-style yogurt. You also add cheese and vanilla and salt. The cheese should be soft goat's cheese. You need 110 g. Use 1 tsp of vanilla and a pinch of salt. Mix all of this together until it is smooth. Pour it carefully into bowls or glasses. It should be enough for four bowls or glasses. Put it in the fridge to chill for an hour. Next you need to make the honey sauce. Put 1 tbsp of sugar into a quarter cup of water in a pan. Add some honey slowly – a tbsp should be enough. Put this in a pan and heat it gently until the sugar dissolves. Leave this to cool. Cut 4 figs neatly in half and put on the panna cotta. Pour on the honey sauce.

You are going to rewrite the recipe so it is easier to understand.

A Planning

1 Ingredients

Read Jafar's recipe sentence by sentence. Make a list of the **ingredients** and the **amounts** he used.

____________________ ____________________

____________________ ____________________

____________________ ____________________

____________________ ____________________

____________________ ____________________

2 Method

Read Jafar's recipe sentence by sentence.

Makes notes on what he did with the ingredients – the **instructions**.

____

____

____

____

____

B Writing

Now use your notes to write the recipe.

Writer's Toolbox

Have you:

- given your recipe a **title**?
- listed the ingredients in the **order** in which they are used?
- used **precise language**?
- put each ingredient on a **new line**?
- written the **method**:
  - in short, clear sentences?
  - in order?
- **numbered** the instructions?
- put each instruction on **a new line**?
- used **imperative verbs**?

Edit and proofread

Correct any mistakes in: spelling punctuation grammar

Write your neat copy.

7 Writing to persuade: advertisements

You will find **advertisements** in magazines and newspapers, on the television, on the internet, and on posters. You will find advertisements **everywhere**!

Advertisements are created to **persuade** people to buy something, do something, join something or visit somewhere.

Let's read

Look at this advertisement for surfboards.

Let's talk

A What does the advertisement tell you? Discuss your answers.

1 What is the advertisement for?

2 What will it give you?

3 Who says that the *Super Sunshine Surfboard* is 'the best there is'?

4 Where can you find more information about the *Super Sunshine Surfboard*?

B Think about advertisements. Discuss your answers.

1 Why do you think people advertise?

2 Who do you think this advertisement is aimed at?

3 Why do you think the advertisement repeats *Super Sunshine Surfboard* so many times?

4 Have you ever persuaded your parents to buy something because you saw it advertised? Explain what was advertised and why the advertisement persuaded you to want it.

C How is an advertisement created? Discuss your answers.

1 Do you think *Super Sunshine Surfboard* is a good name? Why? Why not?

2 Find adjectives that describe:

a the ride b the surfboard.

3 Find the rhyme in the advertisement. Why do you think it includes a rhyme?

4 Why do you think the advertisement includes what the World Champion thinks about the surfboard?

5 Why do you think the advertisement includes a website address and an email address?

6 Do you think the advertisement is attractive? Why, or why not?

Let's learn

Adjectives

Adjectives are describing words.

Advertisements use **powerful adjectives** to **persuade**.

The ride isn't just *nice*, it's ***exhilarating***.

The surfboard isn't just made of *good* materials, it is made of the ***finest*** materials.

A Write a powerful adjective to replace *nice* in each sentence.

1. I had a **nice** day at the beach. ______________________
2. He had a **nice** swim. ______________________
3. The surfboard was **nice**. ______________________
4. The weather was **nice**. ______________________
5. The sea was **nice**. ______________________

Information

Many types of writing need **information**.

The advertisement for Super Sunshine Surfboards gives you information about how to contact them.

For more information visit
www.supersunshinesurfboards.co.oz
or email us at surf@supersunshinesurfboards.co.oz

A Make notes on what other information would be useful in the advertisement.

____

____

____

____

Rhyme

Advertisements are created so that you remember them.

You might remember an advertisement if it has a **slogan**.

A slogan often uses a **rhyme**, so it is easier to remember.

Rhyming words have the same sound.

strong **long**

Some rhyming words are **spelled differently** but sound the same.

light **bite**

A Write some words that rhyme with these words.

1 new ________ ________ ________

________ ________ ________

2 ride ________ ________ ________

________ ________ ________

B Think of your own rhyme to advertise the surfboard.

____

____

Alliteration

Alliteration is when words begin with the **same sound**.

Advertisements often use alliteration.

SUPER SUNSHINE SURFBOARDS

Alliteration helps you remember the name.

A Finish each sentence by adding a word beginning with the same sound as the bold word.

1 I bought a **super**, ________________ surfboard.

2 It was an **exhilarating**, ________________ experience.

3 There were **tall**, ______________________________ waves.

4 This is a **soft**, ______________________________ beach.

5 There was a **brilliant**, ______________________________ sunset.

**B Imagine you are advertising these things.
Add a word beginning with the same sound to each one.**

1 

a ____________________ football

2 

____________________ apples

3 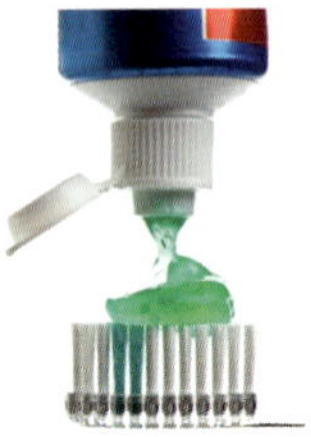

____________________ toothpaste

4 

____________________ trainers

Quotations

A **quotation** is when you repeat the exact words someone has said or written.

The **advertisement** uses a quotation from a World Champion surfer.

The advertisement wants you to think that if the surfboard is good enough for a World Champion, then it's good enough for you!

'If you want to surf like the professionals, then choose the best there is. Choose the **Super Sunshine Surfboard**.' (Joe Manillo – a World Champion surfer)

**A Imagine you have used a Super Sunshine Surfboard and really liked it.
What would you say about it that the advertisers could use in their advertisement?**

____

____

____

B **Imagine you have used a Super Sunshine Surfboard and really hated it! What would you say about it that the advertisers would not use in their advertisement?**

____

____

____

Layout

The way an **advertisement** looks is very important.

People who create advertisements want people to remember them.

They think about:

- how to make sure what is being advertised really stands out
- what colours to use
- the size and colour of the writing
- the illustrations.

A Make notes on:

1 how the advertisers have made Super Sunshine Surfboards stand out

____

____

____

2 the colours and fonts they have used for the writing

____

____

____

3 the illustrations they have chosen for the advertisement.

____

____

____

Let's practise

You are going to create an advertisement for a new drink.

A Planning

1 What is the name of your new drink?

Write some ideas. Think about using alliteration.

Tick the one you like best.

______________________ ☐ ______________________ ☐

______________________ ☐ ______________________ ☐

2 How will you write the name to make it stand out.

____

3 Is your drink in a can or a bottle? can ☐ bottle ☐

4 What is your drink made from?

Does it come in different flavours?

List the ingredients.

______________________ ______________________

______________________ ______________________

5 Who do you think would buy your drink? Who is your advertisement aimed at?

____

6 How will you persuade people to buy your new drink?

Think about:

- powerful adjectives you could use in the advertisement

______________________ ______________________

______________________ ______________________

- information you will need in the advertisement

______________________ ______________________

______________________ ______________________

- a rhyme to help people remember your advertisement

____

____

- a quotation from someone who really liked the drink.

7 What illustration will you use? Make notes.

8 What colours will you use for the writing? You can use different colours for different parts of the advertisement.

9 Use this space to make a rough drawing of your advertisement.

Remember, how it looks is important. Decide:

- where you will put the *name* of your drink
- where you will put the *illustration*
- where you will put the *writing*.

B Writing

Now use your notes and rough drawing to create your advertisement.

Writer's Toolbox

Have you:

- used **alliteration** for the name of your drink?
- made the **name** of your drink **stand out**?
- used **powerful adjectives**?
- included **important information**?
- included a **rhyme**?
- included a **quotation**?
- used an **illustration**?
- made your advertisement **colourful and attractive**?

Edit and proofread

Correct any mistakes in: spelling punctuation grammar

Write your neat copy.

Let's write

You are going to create an advertisement for one of these:

an ice lolly ☐ a magazine about sport ☐ a breakfast cereal ☐

Tick the one you have chosen.

A Planning

Make notes.

1 What is the name of your product? Use alliteration.

____

2 Who is your advertisement aimed at? Who will buy your product?

____

3 How will you persuade people to buy your product?

- Use powerful adjectives. ____________ ____________

____________ ____________

- Include information.

- Include a rhyme.

- Include a quotation.

4 What will be in your illustration?

5 Make a rough drawing of your advertisement here.

B Writing

Now use your notes and rough drawing to create your advertisement.

- Use the **Writer's Toolbox** on page 86.
- **Edit** and **proofread**, correcting mistakes in **spelling**, **punctuation** and **grammar**.
- Write your **neat copy**.

8 Personal writing: recounts

A **recount** is when a writer recounts an **experience** that he or she has had.

Let's read

Read this personal recount about Class 4's trip to an art gallery.

Our Visit to the City Art Gallery

In class, we were studying a famous painting called the *Mona Lisa*. Miss Gill wanted us to see the work of some local artists. On Monday, she arranged a visit to the City Art Gallery.

We arrived at school at the usual time. Miss Gill took the register and then we lined up in the playground. A huge coach arrived at the school gates and we all got in. I was very excited, as I had never been to an art gallery before.

The journey to the gallery took about half an hour as there was a lot of traffic. When we arrived, the driver parked in the car park. We got off the coach and walked to the front steps of the gallery.

Miss Gill told us to gather round her. She told us there would be other people in the gallery and how we had to behave. No running or shouting and no touching! We could look at the paintings but we could not touch them.

Inside the gallery, a young man was waiting for us. He told us his name was Gopal and he worked at the gallery. He handed out clipboards and pencils. On the clipboards was a quiz. We had to walk around the gallery, look at the pictures and find the answers.

The gallery was huge! It had a really high ceiling and loads of paintings on the walls. Some of them were easy to recognise. They were paintings of animals and people, or scenes like forests and mountains. Some of them were very different. They seemed to be big splodges of different colours, or lots of straight lines shooting about. I thought they were very odd.

As I walked around, I did the quiz. It wasn't very difficult. You had to fill in the names of paintings or painters. At the end of the quiz, you had to write the name of your favourite painting and say why you liked it. My favourite was *Lion at Sunset*. A fierce-looking lion was standing in the middle of the painting. It had an enormous yellow mane and its mouth was wide open showing sharp teeth. I could almost hear it roar!

When we had finished looking at the paintings, Gopal asked us if we had enjoyed ourselves. We all said we had a great time. He gave us the answers to the quiz. I got them all right! He then asked us to tell him about our favourite painting. Quite a few of us liked *Lion at Sunset*, but the most popular was a painting that was just red and yellow dots! It was called *Headache*. I thought that was a good name for it as I'm sure I would get a headache if I looked at it for too long! We handed in our clipboards and pencils, said goodbye and thank you to Gopal, and lined up at the door to go back to the coach.

On the journey back, we chatted about our visit to the gallery. Miss Gill said that we would be back in time for lunch. In the afternoon, we were going to make a copy of our favourite painting. It was going to be very difficult for me to paint the lion. I wished I had chosen the one with red and yellow dots!

Let's talk

A What does the personal recount tell you? Discuss your answers.

1 What have the children been studying in class?
2 Who is their teacher?
3 What has the teacher arranged?
4 Who is Gopal?
5 Which is the writer's favourite painting?

B Think about the personal recount. Discuss your answers.

1 How does the writer feel about the visit?
2 Why do you think Miss Gill told them not to run, shout or touch?
3 How does the writer describe the gallery?
4 What does the sentence *I thought they were very odd* tell you about the writer's opinion?
5 How do you know that the writer did not like the painting called *Headache*?

C How is a personal recount written? Discuss your answers.

1 Look at the verbs in the personal recount, for example:

   were studying *arranged* *arrived*

   What tenses are they written in?
2 Why do you think the writer uses the pronouns *I* and *we* in the recount?
3 What questions does the first paragraph answer?
4 How many paragraphs are there?
5 Say briefly what each paragraph is about.

Let's learn

Introduction

The introduction to a **personal recount** gives the reader **information**.

It has a title to say what the recount is about.

Our Visit to the City Art Gallery

It has a **first paragraph** that says:

- where they went — *a visit to the City Art Gallery*
- why they went there. — *We were studying a famous painting called the Mona Lisa. Miss Gill wanted us to see the work of some local artists.*

A Imagine you are writing about a visit to the dentist.

1 Write a sentence to say where you are going.

____

____

____

2 Write a sentence to say why you are going there.

____

____

____

Pronouns – first person

A **personal recount** is written in the **first person**.

It uses the **pronouns I** and **we** because the writer is writing about something that he/she has experienced.

__We__ arrived at school.

__I__ was very excited.

Top Tip

Pronouns are used in place of nouns.

A Write these third-person sentences in the first person.

1 He went to the City Art Gallery.

____

2 They looked at the paintings.

____

3 Miss Gill arranged a visit.

____

4 The children chose their favourite painting.

____

Past tenses

Personal recounts are about something that has happened in the **past**.

They are written in **past tenses**.

The driver __parked__ in the car park.

A fierce-looking lion __was standing__ in the middle of the painting.

A Find and copy six more examples of past tenses in the recount.

1 ____________________ 2 ____________________

3 ____________________ 4 ____________________

5 ____________________ 6 ____________________

B Write these present tense sentences in past tenses.

1 We are walking to the front of the Gallery.

___

2 Gopal works at the Gallery.

___

3 I think that painting is lovely.

___

4 They are doing a quiz.

___

5 We are painting our favourite paintings.

___

Reported speech

Personal recounts don't usually use direct speech.

The writer **reports** what someone has said but:

- does not use the actual spoken words
- does not use speech marks.

Direct speech: *"Did you enjoy yourselves?" asked Gopal.*

Reported speech: *Gopal asked us if we had enjoyed ourselves.*

A Write these direct speech sentences as reported speech.

1 "We are going to visit the City Art Gallery," said Miss Gill.

___

___

2 "I have a quiz for you to do," said Gopal.

___

___

3 "I like painting animals," said the painter.

4 "This quiz is easy," he said.

5 "We are going to do some painting," said Miss Gill.

Order

A **personal recount** is about something the writer has experienced.

The best way to write it is to **start at the beginning** and write about the things that happened in **the order they happened**.

The personal recount *Our Visit to the City Art Gallery* is written **in order**:

- where the writer was going and why
- what happened when everyone arrived at school
- the journey to the gallery
- outside the gallery
- inside the gallery
- the journey back to school.

Fact and opinion

Personal recounts have:

- facts — *We arrived at school at the usual time.*

  The Gallery was huge!
- the writer's opinions — *I thought they were very odd.*

  My favourite was Lion at Sunset.

A **Look carefully at this famous painting.**

It was painted by Vincent Van Gogh.

It is called *Sunflowers*.

B **Write three facts about the painting.**

1 ______________________________

____

2 ______________________________

____

3 ______________________________

____

C **Write what you think of the painting – your opinion.**

____

____

____

Let's practise

You have read a **recount** about Class 4's visit to an art gallery.

They were studying famous painters so Miss Gill arranged the visit to help the children with their work.

The recount was written by one of the children who went on the visit.

You are going to write a personal recount about a visit you have made with your class.

A Planning

Use the questions below to help you plan your recount. Make notes.

1 Where did you visit? ___

2 Why did your teacher arrange this visit?

___

___

___

3 When did the visit happen? ___

4 Who went on the visit? Did another class or teacher come with you?

___

___

___

5 How did you feel about going on the visit? ___

___

___

6 How did you travel to the place? ___

___

7 What did you see on the visit? ___

___

___

___

8 What was your opinion of what you saw? ______________________

____

____

9 What did you do on the visit? ______________________

____

____

10 How did you feel when it had finished? ______________________

____

____

B Writing

Now use your notes to write your personal recount.

Give it a title.

Writer's Toolbox

Have you:

- made it clear in the **introduction**:
  - **where** you went?
  - **why** you went there?
- used **first person pronouns**?
- written in **past tenses**?
- used **reported speech**?
- written things in the **order** that they happened?
- included **facts**?
- included your **opinions**?

Edit and proofread

Correct any mistakes in: spelling punctuation grammar

Write your neat copy.

Let's write

You are going to write a personal recount of a place you have visited. The visit could have been with friends or family.

A Planning

1 Where did you visit?

Choose one of these and tick the box next to it, or choose your own idea and write it out in the space below.

☐ the cinema ☐ the park ☐ a famous building ☐ the seaside

____

2 Why did you visit this place?

Was it a special occasion? Were you on holiday? Were you meeting someone?

____

____

3 Who went on the visit?

____

____

4 How did you feel about going on the visit? Excited? Bored? Worried? Something else?

____

____

5 How did you travel to the place?
By car or train? By walking or cycling? In some other way?

____

6 What did you see and do on the visit?
Makes notes of the facts and your opinions.

Facts	Opinions
______________	______________
______________	______________
______________	______________
______________	______________

7 How did you feel when the visit was over?

Was it better or worse than you expected? Why?

B Writing

Now use your notes to write your personal recount.

Give it a title.

Writer's Toolbox

Have you:

- made it clear in the **introduction**:
  - **where** you went
  - **why** you went there?
- used **first person pronouns**?
- written in **past tenses**?
- used **reported speech**?
- written things in the **order** that they happened?
- included **facts**?
- included your **opinions**?

Edit and proofread

Correct any mistakes in: spelling punctuation grammar

Write your neat copy.

9 Narrative writing: play scripts

Play scripts are the words actors say in a play.

Let's read

Read the first scene of this play called *The Mystery of Sol*.

The Mystery of Sol

Characters

Miss Layla				*the teacher*
Sol	Ava	Lonny	Cherie	*schoolchildren*

Scene 1: **At school**

The children are in class. Sol and Lonny are new at the school. Ever since they arrived, Ava has been watching them. They are acting strangely.

Miss Layla: There is going to be a test. Put away your books.

Sol: *[to himself while looking all around]* Where do I put my books? I can't see where the other students have put their books.

Ava: *[whispering]* They go under here. Look, on the shelf under your desk. Haven't you sat at a desk before?

Sol: *[embarrassed]* Of course I have. Oh…yes, I know what to do.

The test begins.

Sol: *[to Lonny]* I've finished the test. Let's go.

Lonny: Okay. *[Lonny and Sol leave the classroom.]*

Ava: *[whispering to Cherie]* Where are those two going? The test doesn't finish for another ten minutes. They didn't even ask Miss Layla if they could leave.

Cherie: *[whispering]* I don't know. They don't seem to understand how things work in school.

Miss Layla: Ava, go and bring Sol and Lonny back into the classroom.

Ava leaves and runs down the hallway.

Ava: Where are you going?

Sol: I finished the test. I was going to have some tea.

Ava: *[surprised]* You can't just leave the classroom for tea whenever you want. You have to wait for the teacher to say you can go.

Sol: *[confused]* Why? I had finished the test.

Ava: Yes, but that's not how school works. There are rules.

Lonny: How do these rules work? Tell me about them.

Ava: What do you mean? They work like the rules in all schools. What was it like at your old school?

Sol: At my old school, we did things differently.

Lonny: Yes, my old school was very different from this one, too.

Ava: But you must have had rules. All schools have rules.

Sol: Yes, of course we had rules. In etiquette class we learned about rules. We learned who you bow to and which fork to use when you sit down to dinner. Yes, we had lots of rules. Everywhere you looked was another rule.

Ava: *[surprised]* Forks? Bowing? What is this etiquette class you're talking about? We don't have classes like that. We don't have a class to learn about rules. We're just supposed to know them. Like you should know that if you have to leave the classroom, you must ask the teacher first. You can't just get up from your seat and leave.

Lonny: Okay, I understand it now. We must follow the rules. We didn't learn that at our old school. We won't make that mistake again.

Ava: *[confused]* But I thought you two came from different schools. I thought you met here.

Lonny: *[nervously]* Yes… yes, we went to different schools in very different places. But it looks as if both schools failed to teach us the right rules. But we know now, thanks to you. What's your name?

Ava: My name's Ava.

Sol: Thank you so very much, Ava. You have helped us a lot.

Let's talk

A What happens in the play? Discuss your answers.

1 Why do the students have to put away their books?

2 What does Sol do when he finishes?

3 What don't Sol and Lonny do before they leave the classroom?

4 What does Miss Layla tell Ava to do?

5 What did Sol learn in etiquette class?

B What do we learn about the characters? Discuss your answers.

1 Who are the characters in the play?

2 What does Cherie think about Sol and Lonny?

3 What do we know about Sol?

4 What do we know about Ava?

C How is a play script written? Discuss your answers.

1 How do you know that the scene takes place at school?

2 On the page, where are:

  a the characters' names?

  b the words they say?

3 How are the stage directions written?

4 Find a stage direction that tells an actor:

  a how to say something

  b what to do.

Let's learn

Contractions

Characters in plays are **speaking** to each other.

When we speak we often use short forms of words. We say:

can't for cannot   **haven't** for have not   **I've** for I have

These are called **contractions**.

They have an **apostrophe** for the missing letters.

Use contractions when you write dialogue in play scripts.

Top Tip

To contract means to get smaller.

A Find five more contractions in the play script.

Write each contraction. Then write the long form of each contraction.

	Contraction	Long form
1	____________________	____________________
2	____________________	____________________
3	____________________	____________________
4	____________________	____________________
5	____________________	____________________

Dialogue in play scripts

Dialogue in play scripts does **not** have speech marks.

We know when a character is speaking because their name is written before the words they say.

In a **story** we write:

"Where are you going?" asked Ava.

In a **play script** we write:

Ava: *Where are you going?*

A Find and write the names of the characters who say these words in the play script.

1 There is going to be a test. Put away your books. ______________________

2 Yes, but that's not how school works. There are rules. ______________________

3 At my old school, we did things differently. ______________________

B Set out this conversation as a play script.

"You know those two new boys," said Ava.
"Sol and Lonny?" asked Cherie.
"Yes, those two," replied Ava.
"What about them?" asked Cherie.
"Well," said Ava, "don't you think they are acting strangely?"
"What do you mean?" asked Cherie.
"They don't seem to know how a school works!" exclaimed Ava.

Character	Dialogue
______________________	____
______________________	____
______________________	____
______________________	____
______________________	____
______________________	____
______________________	____

The layout of play scripts

The **layout** of a play script is different from a story and other pieces of writing.

A play script must include:

- a **title**
- a list of **characters** – the people in the play
- the **number of the scene** – if there is more than one scene
- some information about where **the scene is set**
- **dialogue** – what the characters say
- **stage directions** – words and phrases to tell an actor how to speak.

A Look at the play again.

1 What is the title of the play? ______________________

2 Who are the characters in the play?

______________ ______________ ______________

______________ ______________

3 What is the number of the scene? ______________________

4 Where is the scene set? ______________________

5 Find and copy a short piece of dialogue.

____

____

6 Find and copy a stage direction. ______________________

7 Are the characters' names on the left or right of the page? ______________________

8 Is the dialogue on the left or right of the page? ______________________

9 How are the stage directions written? ______________________

10 Do the actors say the stage directions? ______________________

Let's practise

This could be the beginning of the **next scene** of the play. Miss Layla has started the lesson when Sol and Lonny walk in. They are very late.

Miss Layla: *[annoyed] You are very late!*

Sol: *I thought the lesson would begin when I arrived.*

You are going to write the next scene of the play.

A Planning

Use the questions below to help you plan the scene. Make notes.

1 Who are the characters in the scene?

_______________ _______________ _______________

_______________ _______________

2 What number scene is this? Scene _______________

3 Where is the scene set?

____

____

4 Miss Layla says the lesson does not begin when Sol arrives.

Write what she says.

Write a stage direction in the brackets to show how she says it.

[_______________] _______________

____

5 Sol explains that, in his old school, the lesson began when he arrived.

Write what he says.

Write a stage direction in the brackets to show how he says it.

[_______________] _______________

____

6 Miss Layla asks one of the children to explain to Sol about when a lesson begins. Who does she ask? Tick one.

Ava ☐ Cherie ☐

What does the character say?

Write a stage direction to show how she says it.

[______________________] ____

____

7 What does Sol say?

Write a stage direction to show how he says it.

[______________________] ____

____

8 Does Sol apologise to Miss Layla?

What does he say?

Write a stage direction to show how he says it.

[______________________] ____

____

B Writing

Now use your notes to write the scene.

Writer's Toolbox

Have you:

- written a list of the **characters**?
- **numbered** the scene?
- explained where the **scene is set**?
- written the **characters' names on the left**?
- written the **dialogue on the right**?
- used **contractions** in the dialogue?
- used **stage directions** to show how a character says the words?

Edit and proofread

Correct any mistakes in: spelling punctuation grammar

Write your neat copy.

Let's write

The **next scene** of the play takes place in the playground. It is break time.

Some children are kicking a football. Some are standing in groups talking.

Sol and Lonny think it is the end of the school day. They are walking through the gates when Cherie catches up with them.

You are going to write the next scene of the play.

A Planning

Use the questions below to help you plan the scene. Make notes.

1 What number scene is this? Scene ______________________

2 Where is the scene set?

____

____

3 Who are the characters in the scene? You can add other characters.

______________ ______________ ______________

______________ ______________ ______________

4 What does Cherie ask Sol and Lonny at the gates?

Write what she asks. Write how she says it.

[______________] ______________________________

____

5 Sol explains he is going home.

Write what he says. Write how he says it.

[______________] ______________________________

____

6 Cherie asks why he is going home.

What does she say? Write how she says it.

[______________] ______________________________

____

7 What does Sol say? Write how he says it.

[________________] ______________________________

____

8 How does Cherie explain that he cannot go home?

What does she say?

Write how she says it.

[________________] ______________________________

____

B Writing

Now use your notes to write the scene.

Writer's Toolbox

Have you:

- written a list of the **characters**?
- **numbered** the scene?
- explained where the scene is **set**?
- written the **characters' names on the left**?
- written the **dialogue on the right**?
- used **contractions** in the dialogue?
- used **stage directions** to show how a character says the words?

Edit and proofread

Correct any mistakes in: spelling punctuation grammar

Write your neat copy.

Stage 4 Unit 1 assessment sheet

Book blurbs: my favourite story

Everyone has a favourite story.

It might be one that was read to you when you were very young.

It might be one that you have read yourself.

You are going to write a book blurb for your favourite story.

Write the name of your favourite story. ____________________________

Here is your book blurb Writer's Toolbox.

Writer's Toolbox

	Tick
• Include the **main points** of the story.	☐
• Mention the **main characters**.	☐
• Write in **present tenses**.	☐
• Keep the blurb **short**.	☐
• Mainly use **short sentences**.	☐
• Do not **give away the ending**.	☐
• End with **a question**.	☐

1 Write your first draft.

2 Read through the Toolbox. Tick the tools you have used.

3 If you have **four or more ticks**, colour in the smiley face.

4 Can you make changes to your first draft to get more ticks?

5 Correct mistakes in spelling, punctuation and grammar.

6 Write your neat copy.

Stage 4 Unit 2 assessment sheet

Characters in stories: the shopkeeper

Mr Aziz is the local shopkeeper and all the people in the neighbourhood use his shop.

It is early in the morning and Mr Aziz is opening the shop and putting the baskets of fresh fruit and vegetables outside.

You are going to write a character description of Mr Aziz.

You need to:

- describe what he looks like
- describe his personality.

Here is your character description Writer's Toolbox.

Writer's Toolbox

	Tick
• Use **capital letters** for proper nouns.	☐
• Use **pronouns** so you do not have to keep repeating *Mr Aziz*.	☐
• Write in **past tenses**.	☐
• Use **adjectives** to describe his physical appearance:	☐
– what does he **look like?**	
– what is he **wearing?**	
• Describe his **personality**.	☐
• Use adverbs to show how he **acts** and **speaks**.	☐

1. Write your first draft.
2. Read through the Toolbox. Tick the tools you have used.
3. If you have **three or more ticks**, colour in the smiley face.
4. Can you make changes to your first draft to get more ticks?
5. Correct mistakes in spelling, punctuation and grammar.
6. Write your neat copy.

Stage 4 Unit 3 assessment sheet

Acrostics and haikus: raindrop

An **acrostic** is a form of poem where the first letter of each line spells a word.

A **haiku** has three lines:

1st line = 5 syllables   2nd line = 7 syllables   3rd line = 5 syllables

You are going to write an acrostic or a haiku, using the word

R A I N D R O P

Here is your acrostic Writer's Toolbox.

Writer's Toolbox

	Tick
• Start each line with the **correct letter**.	☐
• Use interesting **adjectives**.	☐
• Use **sentences**, **phrases** and **single words**.	☐

Here is your haiku Writer's Toolbox.

Writer's Toolbox

	Tick
• Use only **three lines**.	☐
• Use **five syllables** in Line 1.	☐
• Use **seven syllables** in Line 2.	☐
• Use **five syllables** in Line 3.	☐

1 Write your first draft.

2 Read through the Toolbox. Tick the tools you have used.

3 If you have **two or more ticks**, colour in the smiley face.

4 Can you make changes to your first draft to get more ticks?

5 Correct mistakes in spelling, punctuation and grammar.

6 Write your neat copy.

Stage 4 Unit 4 assessment sheet
Factual report: an amazing place

When you find out the **facts** about a subject and put them in a piece of writing, you produce a **factual report**.

You are going to write a factual report about one of these.

Pyramid of Cheops

The Batu Caves

Here is your factual report Writer's Toolbox.

Writer's Toolbox

	Tick
• Research the **facts**.	☐
• Make **notes**.	☐
• Order your notes into **paragraphs**.	☐
• Write a **first sentence** to make it clear what the report is about.	☐
• Give your report a **title**.	☐

1 Write your first draft.

2 Read through the Toolbox. Tick the tools you have used.

3 If you have **three or more ticks**, colour in the smiley face.

4 Can you make changes to your first draft to get more ticks?

5 Correct mistakes in spelling, punctuation and grammar.

6 Write your neat copy.

Stage 4 Unit 5 assessment sheet
Dialogue in stories: talking with your friend

Characters in stories talk to each other.

They have a **conversation**.

We talk to lots of different people throughout the day about lots of different things.

You are going to write a conversation between you and your friend. Choose one of these topics for your conversation.

school **sport** **television**

Here is your conversation Writer's Toolbox.

Writer's Toolbox

	Tick
• Put **speech marks** around the spoken words.	
• Use a **comma** between the spoken and non-spoken words.	
• Use a **capital letter** for the first word spoken.	
• Use a **question mark** for a question.	
• Use an **exclamation mark** for an exclamation.	
• Use **contractions**.	
• Use **synonyms** for said.	
• Use **split direct speech**.	

1 Write your first draft.

2 Read through the Toolbox. Tick the tools you have used.

3 If you have **five or more ticks**, colour in the smiley face.

4 Can you make changes to your first draft to get more ticks?

5 Correct mistakes in spelling, punctuation and grammar.

6 Write your neat copy.

Stage 4 Unit 6 assessment sheet
Instructions: making a sandwich

Sandwiches are very popular.

They can be made from different types of bread.

They can have different fillings.

Some sandwiches are savoury and some are sweet.

You are going to write a set of instructions for making your favourite sandwich.
You need to think about:

- **the ingredients you need**
- **the order in which you use the ingredients.**

Here is your instructions Writer's Toolbox.

Writer's Toolbox

	Tick
• Give your instructions a **title**.	☐
• Write a **list** of ingredients.	☐
• Use **precise language**.	☐
• Put each ingredient on a **new line**.	☐
• Write the method in **short, clear sentences**.	☐
• Write the method **in order**.	☐
• **Number** the instructions.	☐
• Write each instruction on a **new line**.	☐
• Use **imperative verbs**.	☐

1 Write your first draft.

2 Read through the Toolbox. Tick the tools you have used.

3 If you have **five or more ticks**, colour in the smiley face.

4 Can you make changes to your first draft to get more ticks?

5 Correct mistakes in spelling, punctuation and grammar.

6 Write your neat copy.

Stage 4 Unit 7 assessment sheet
Advertisements: a new toothpaste

A company called *Feel Fresh* has invented a new toothpaste.

It is for young children.

They have made it taste really good.

You are going to create an advertisement for the new toothpaste.
You need to think about:

- **a great name for the toothpaste**
- **what the tube looks like.**

Here is your advertisement Writer's Toolbox.

Writer's Toolbox

	Tick
• Use **alliteration** for the name.	☐
• Make the name of the toothpaste **stand out** in the advertisement.	☐
• Use **powerful adjectives**.	☐
• Include important **information**.	☐
• Include a **rhyme**.	☐
• Include a **quotation**.	☐
• Include an **illustration**.	☐
• Make your advertisement **colourful and attractive**.	☐

1 Write your first draft.

2 Read through the Toolbox. Tick the tools you have used.

3 If you have **four or more ticks**, colour in the smiley face.

4 Can you make changes to your first draft to get more ticks?

5 Correct mistakes in spelling, punctuation and grammar.

6 Write your neat copy

Stage 4 Unit 8 assessment sheet

Personal recounts: a journey to a strange planet

HaHa is a strange planet very far from Earth.
A rocket called *Adventure* left Earth a long time ago.
It landed and explored the planet HaHa.
The crew returned safely to Earth.
Imagine you were one of the crew.

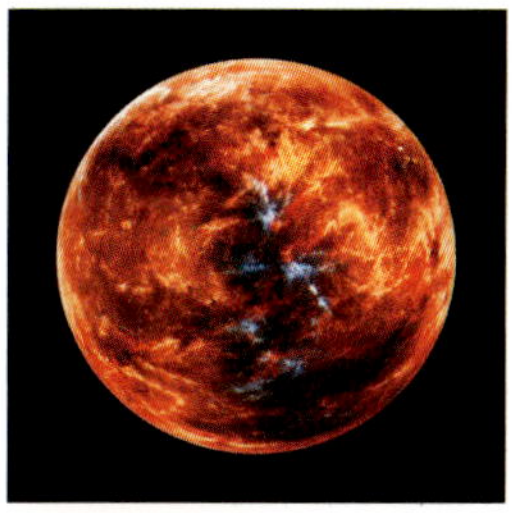

You are going to write a personal recount of your time on the planet. Begin like this:

***Adventurer* landed gently on the surface of the planet. We looked out onto a strange new world.**

Here is your personal recount Writer's Toolbox.

Writer's Toolbox

	Tick
• Give your recount a **title**.	☐
• Write a clear **introduction** to say:	
– **where** you went	☐
– **why** you went there	☐
• Use **first person pronouns**.	☐
• Write in **past tenses**.	☐
• Use **reported speech**.	☐
• Write the things that happened on the visit **in order**.	☐
• Include **facts**.	☐
• Include your **opinions**.	☐

1 Write your first draft.
2 Read through the Toolbox. Tick the tools you have used.
3 If you have **five or more ticks**, colour in the smiley face.
4 Can you make changes to your first draft to get more ticks?
5 Correct mistakes in spelling, punctuation and grammar.
6 Write your neat copy.

Stage 4 Unit 9 assessment sheet
Play scripts: the spelling test

Ayesha and two of her friends are in the playground.

They are talking about their next lesson.

They are going to have a spelling test.

Ayesha has forgotten about the test!

You are going to write your conversation about the spelling test as a play scene.
You need to:

- **list the characters**
- **set the scene**
- **write the dialogue.**

Here is your play script Writer's Toolbox.

Writer's Toolbox

	Tick
• Write a list of the **characters**.	☐
• **Number** the scene.	☐
• Explain where the **scene is set**.	☐
• Write the **characters' names on the left**.	☐
• Write the **dialogue on the right**.	☐
• Use **contractions** in the dialogue.	☐
• Use **stage directions** to show how a character says the words.	☐

1 Write your first draft.

2 Read through the Toolbox. Tick the tools you have used.

3 If you have **four or more ticks**, colour in the smiley face.

4 Can you make changes to your first draft to get more ticks?

5 Correct mistakes in spelling, punctuation and grammar.

6 Write your neat copy.

Acknowledgements

The authors and publishers acknowledge the following sources of copyright material and are grateful for the permissions granted. While every effort has been made, it has not always been possible to identify the sources of all the material used, or to trace all copyright holders. If any omissions are brought to our notice, we will be happy to include the appropriate acknowledgements on reprinting.

Stephen Frink /Getty Images; H. Armstrong Roberts/ClassicStock/Getty Images; Severin Sadjina - sesaphoto.com/Getty Images; portishead1/Getty Images; Manoj Shah/Getty Images; Fraser Hall/Getty Images; Aaron Foster/Getty Images; Akepong Srichaichana / EyeEm/Getty Images; Jeff Greenberg/UIG/Getty Images; Billy Richards Photography/ Getty Images; Ed Norton/Getty Images; John Harper/Getty Images; Iain Masterton/Getty Images; John Short / Design Pics/Getty Images; Ramesan Kuyyalil / EyeEm/Getty Images; aiqingwang/Getty Images; Fraser Hall/Getty Images; Posnov/Getty Images; HAGENS WORLD PHOTOGRAPHY/Getty Images; Jeremy Woodhouse/Getty Images; RAZVAN CIUCA/ Getty Images; Nasrul Effendy / EyeEm/Getty Images; Tanatat pongphibool ,thailand/ Getty Images; NASA/Getty Images; Bettmann/Getty Images; NASA/Getty Images; Foodcollection RF/Getty Images; paylessimages/Getty Images; MarkGillow/Getty Images; Steve Brown Photography/Getty Images; Marco Simoni/Getty Images; Warren Bolster/ Getty Images; Warren Bolster/Getty Images; acrylik/Getty Images; xxmmxx/Getty Images; DebbiSmirnoff/Getty Images; DonNichols/Getty Images; Science Photo Library/Getty Images; Picture Finders Ltd/Getty Images; Universal History Archive/Getty Images; Jeff Overs/Getty Images; Nick Brundle Photography/Getty Images; Nick Brundle Photography/ Getty Images; Dan Goldberg/Getty Images;